WHO'S GOING TO LOVE THE DYING GIRL?

BREE ROLFE

Attention schools and businesses: for discounted copies on large orders, please contact the publisher directly. Retailers and libraries can order copies through Ingram

Unsolicited Press
Portland, Oregon
www.unsolicitedpress.com
info@unsolicitedpress.com
619-354-8005

Cover Design: Kathryn Gerhardt
Editor: Samuel Nichols; Bekah Stogner
ISBN: 978-1-950730-77-3

TABLE OF CONTENTS

For Bonnie Staiger who first gifted me this life filled with words

A LITANY OF BAD DECISIONS

PART ONE: OMENS

The only remaining
correspondence between
the two of us— a *New York
Times* article about Marfa
and a reply of *yippee*.

Jon Krakauer's *Under the Banner
of Heaven* on audiobook—
Mormonism, blood
atonement, a six hour
drive through desert.

The first gallery with photographs
of Katrina's destruction paired
with poems by children left
in her wake. Something beautiful
repurposed from storm
but still destruction.

PART TWO: TAKE IT ALL BACK

Some farm-to-table restaurant
with a name that involved
chicken and electricity
where you bring your own wine.
A loud table of sophisticated

middle-aged couples, tipsy and deep,
deep in conversation. Us, silent,
draining everything we brought.

A bar afterwards, a folk singer
finishes his set and we talk
too long about Club Passim.

We meet a couple, and you tell them
you're from Brooklyn and I say,
but you're from Connecticut.
All of your drinks on my tab—
scotches piled upon scotches.

Then, a Milky Way-themed trailer
that sells grilled cheese—
you screaming at me from a bean bag
chair, everything misshapen
in black light, and so twisted, I walk out
and back to our rental alone
through pitch-black streets
with no real sidewalks.

Who's going to love the dying girl?

It all unravels: a smashed phone,
a disconnected call, an overturned
coffee table, a locked bathroom,
chunks of my hair, unmoored.

PART THREE: AFTERMATH

Triplicates of paperwork.
A gas stop, a guy on a Harley
with a sympathetic look,
and then cheap sunglasses.

A legion of bugs sacrificed
on my windshield with no substance
in the world other than sheer
will to scrub them off.

Six hours to forget:

I'll leave you in a shallow
grave in West Texas.

THE SPLIT SECOND WHERE IT BEGINS AND SPLINTERS OUTWARD

There is that sharp moment
when you first feel pain—
when the initial sting stabs
through your nerves and turns
into everything you've ever done
wrong in your entire life, distilled
into a tangible throbbing.

In the photograph the cop took,
it begins with a few slashes of red,
a puffing, *not that bad.*
The next day, everything is
deepening; swirls murk
green and purple.

I think about that scene in *Mask*
where Rocky is trying to teach
the blind girl about color.
She's been blind since birth—
has no concept of what colors mean.

He wants to show her—
leads her to the kitchen, heats up
a stone, places it into her unsuspecting
hand and says *this is red.*
He takes another stone
from the freezer and says

this is blue and for *green,*
he presses a clump of moss
into her open palms.

He puts her own hands
to her face and says, *beautiful.*
When she asks to feel his disfigured
face, he hesitates, then relents.
She says, *feels okay to me.*

I used to think this moment
when she presses the contours
of his face, was perfection;
now, I want her to be able to see
his face and still say it's okay.

Later, on my own face, I touch
where yellow slights
along edges. And I can't
remember exactly what hit
and where and at what angles.

SPACE

Morning in this place—
piles of pillows,
the sun barely breaks
through patchwork
curtains, throwing waves
of light across the floor.

In this place, only the curtains
create divisions, each door opens
into another—there could never
be anywhere alone.

On the porch, someone else's
husband is reading a yellowed book.
I hear him say the walls are paper thin—
He thinks I've heard everything
they've said all night, but I haven't.

The space of my life is always
this way— spent oscillating
between trying to be and not wanting
to be alone— that wedge of space

like the one in the corner of the kitchen
in the house where I grew up—
A triangle of space, formed
by a Lazy Susan cabinet,
where Evan Ferguson, a foot taller,
bent in half to kiss me.

Blonde hair flopping over one eye,
wearing the blue shirt that turned
his eyes so blue, they felt electric.
He smelled like laundry,
even though he was sweaty
from skateboarding.

This is what's most vivid—
that space— that corner, me slotted
into that corner, a spinning
cabinet where we kept all the spices.

And now it seems like we were
supposed to fit— two bodies,
folded in a corner. Outside,
our friends were jumping
on a trampoline. We could hear
them screaming.

LOOKING AT A FRIEND'S PHOTOGRAPHS OF THE SALTON SEA THE MORNING AFTER HE KILLED HIMSELF

If landscape acts as message—

Half dug in, half resigned,
Disney TVs leaning on bluish ground
with bullet-splintered screens
and heart-shaped buttons.

The shell of an easy chair—reclining
on the bland shoreline, water the color of whiskey.
It leans back like it's about to let go,
about to slump into the stagnant
water and sink into stupor.

A washed-out yellow house, *soon,* in graffiti—
a warning emblazoned on its chest.
Its roof rounded like a disfigured birthday cake
baked too long in this ruthless sun.
The row of windows like waiting eyes.

Turn the corner, along the side of the house—
sun slants, cuts shadows into concrete, while above

curlicue words stretch, whispering, *everything must end*
and interrupt beach-weathered wood.

Trailers peel apart, piled with dismantled chain
link fences— air conditioners invade
sleeping areas. The car that once pulled it, unhitched.

A FEW SECONDS TO ANSWER

The sun came up with no conclusions—
spattering emptiness across our faces.
I gave up in the driving sand.

And what we felt was regret.

If we were lions, there would be
rules— postures we could mime.

We would play the game
and feel powerful. But in between,
everything feels like Jeopardy,
where there is an impossible
question and only a few
seconds to answer it correctly.

We are useless like cat massage
living in the house where you grew up,
clinging to common calculations,
drowning in wall-to -wall what ifs.

But the day we climbed like baby
birds out of the sunroof

of my Toyota Corolla listening
to Mazzy Star on repeat—
that day was something else.

THE LOBSTER

Nigel regrets his rap days.
I make mixes of emo songs I loved
ten years ago.

In Texas, he's divorced
and I'm dying.

But back home— there's him
in a tracksuit performing
in Kim Shorey's basement.

And then, there's me loving it.
I'm Rob Base and I came to get down...

This is what adults do—

drink too much
stay up too late
steep in nostalgia.

But what if we could operate
in some other space?

Between the gray area

where people still send letters
and steal bowling balls.

Once, we tried
to set a grocery store lobster free.

He hid it
in his trench coat.

We left it for someone
who owned a saltwater tank.

In the morning,
the guy called and asked,
did you leave a dead
lobster in my car?

What if we are the place
where good intentions go awry?

SOMEWHERE BETWEEN WATERCOLOR AND NOTHING AT ALL

We're a parasitic mess—
    though who is sponging
        who is not clear.

We're murky, a swirl of mean

                        tentacles
                        scratching
                        entwined.

                                    Pushing away.

You: a bar in Chatham,
screaming into your phone.

Middle-aged mothers asking
                        you to meet them
                        on the beach
                        after they put their kids
                        to bed.

Sifting through offers of ugly sex and cocaine
            you invited only
                    so you could turn them down.

The cocktail parties
soccer moms

who hug you too long,
too tight

you're sure it means they want to fuck you.

And there's me:

weaving

through

isles of books,
trying to find the one

to ease my methhead ex's mind.

One that will make him

stand still
and listen

Me,
sneaking

beers in the back,
pretending to be
supportive sober
driving us home
half-drunk.

When you disappear

back
into radio
silence

like so many retreating
satellites sent out
and forgotten—

It is quieter.

The static gone.

But there on the edges,
Something light and pretty.

The palest watercolor
on construction paper.

A blinking pink neon
sign in a hotel lobby

that says: *fine.*

ORGANS II

If we had known then
that it wasn't the London air
or the cocaine—

That the bad was coming
from somewhere much deeper:
thickening fluids trapped
microorganisms until they became
hostile and restless, banding
together into dangerous colonies.

It was coming from somewhere
tiny, some unfortunate ripple in code—

a reaction that began,
in small ways, in London,
but in even smaller ways before then.

I could never hold my breath
underwater for the entire length
of the pool like my sister.

Maybe it might've been heard,
if we'd listened closely,
actually paid attention.

Or maybe we could've heard it
if we hadn't clomped
in our tap shoes on the street

even though we were told
not to wear them outside
because they'd get ruined.

Maybe if I had stopped
climbing from the crib,
jumping down onto organ keys

they would have heard
my sleepy breaths,
whispering warnings.

Or maybe when we screamed
along to that *Really Rosie* record
and Carole King sang,
You'd better believe me
I'm a great big deal
she was trying to tell us.
But would we have listened?

SIMON TELLS ME THE STORY OF HIS CALCULATOR

and the day that he brought it
to his elementary school classroom.
His excitement about the tricks he could
do was too earnest. His neediness vibrating
too visibly on his fingertips. The calculator
now symbolic for an abrupt shift in his social life.

But some things wait to become problems:
habits and consequences disconnected—
a dorm room permeated with too many cloves
and boys, boys huddling by the dumpster
smoking weed in the winter and so much smoke.

Even you weren't rotten at first—
The irony of the Christmas Eve we met,
free shots of whiskey passed from old friend
to old friend. I looked at you under
twinkling lights and thought, *nothing bad
can ever come from that face.*

Now, a ghost face on my chest x-ray peeks
out between the third rib with an O-mouth
resting on the fourth, cartoonish

in the way it draws attention to itself,
but so ridiculous that I'm not even really sure
it's there, and I am too afraid to ask.

Days later, Simon is crying in my classroom,
telling me that everyone who gets to know him
gets sick of him, that he eventually
wears them out, becomes *too much*.
He says, *it's gradual, but it always happens.*

AGAPITÓS

My grandfather forgot how to speak
Greek after his first stroke. When he wandered,
the cops would pull him over and he'd tell them
he was trying to find his mother's grave,
as if their language was buried with her.

What I've lost is tangible— short breaths
forced out at a rapid pace, measured
on a graph detailing falling numbers.
What I've forgotten how to do
charted as a rate of steady decline.
What matters is, I can no longer sing

along with the radio. No longer have the breath
to scream Op Ivy at the top of my lungs:
All I know is that I don't know nothing…

But forgetting how to love you wasn't hard—
it was like losing the words to R.E.M's
It's the End of the World as We Know It—

a barrage, spit too fast, said and fading
in such speed it was hard to tell
if they even existed at all.

Forgetting was so easy, even Michael Stipe
handed a lyric sheet to someone
at every concert and asked them to check.

But there was no one to check us—
no lyric sheet to go by.

Sometimes, I wonder if it's like forgetting
that the Trash Can Sinatras even existed
until one of their songs comes on the radio.
Suddenly, everything feels good again—
something familiar washing over me,
warm water after being out in the cold.

Or the way my grandfather found the Greek
word for *beloved* etched on his mother's
grave, after they told him it wasn't where
he remembered it was and that it was somewhere
else he couldn't ever get to, no matter how
much he searched or how long he dug.

THE EVER-LIVING GHOST OF WHAT ONCE WAS... *

Imagine, Tom Petty and my mother,
the same age, sharing a Scorpion Bowl
in whatever semblance of heaven
I've assembled to make myself feel better.

There was the day on our front steps
when I was eight, where she stepped
on a grasshopper I told her to avoid.
She didn't listen and crushed it.
When I flipped, my father said,
Gayle, she tried to tell you.

I built a house for that grasshopper
out of a matchbox, but really, who has
an actual matchbox for wooden matches?

Is there a ghost in my house?

One night, I came home with my friends—
completely high, maybe drunk
as she backed her Toyota Camry out
of the driveway to look for my father.
I leaned into the driver's side window,

expecting to be in trouble,
but she said, *go into the house.*
I'll be back. Everything is going to be okay.

A few days later, I came home at dawn, tripping
with fresh, hot donuts from the grocery store.
My dad left without a word because he had
traffic and manual labor
to deal with. My mother, heading
to the hospital where she worked,
muttered something like, *you're going
to get it when I get home.*

But I decided that morning, in a fog
of dough and acid, I am an adult.
If I want to come home at six am
with my dude friends, then *it's fine.*

We huddled in the basement.
Watched *Troll 2* out of pinhole eyes—
freaked out and *in love,*
like when you're night swimming
and remember there's a dead cow
at the bottom of John's Pond

or that you got away with being fucked
up because your dad was cheating
on your mom. That no one noticed
you were crying in that sliver
of a bathroom or that you were making
out in the backyard with a boy
who had a prison tattoo of some other
girl's name or that the trampoline
had a tear halfway through it and soon,
someone would fall through, break something,
and it would totally be all your fault.

from "No One's Gonna Love You More Than I Do" by Band of Horses

PROVIDENCE

There's a sign
in the lobby that reads:

Fine

in unblinking neon.

The day before you arrive,
I don't notice.

After you're gone,
it's there— suddenly constant,
freakishly pink.

The hotel bartender
from Kansas tells me
he builds large scale
sculptures.

He's trying to reconstruct
the one-room schoolhouse
his mother taught in
on a field outside
Providence.

Later, you and I will run
through a downpour
back to this bar where
you'll tell me you changed

your mind, then turn
me around and push me
into an elevator.

You'll say: *I don't want to
share your attention.*

I want to tell you:
I know about parasites.

Or maybe, *I know how
the body can betray itself.*

Ten years ago,
a San Francisco hotel
in a twin bed:

I remember the texture
of your undershirt
and a shaking so slight,
I might've imagined it.

I want to say:
*I understand
how a body can tell the truth.*

Even when you don't
want it to— even
when you try to force it not to—

It won't lie.
It won't let you lie.

MAINE/ MONTREAL

We went to Montreal— okay, so it was
Maine, but there was a cobblestone square—
We walked through it late at night.

You and I on a hotel bed. And the fight
that made everything over.
Or the one you still say is the end.

And in the photographs on the wall,
I could see it— *Pavement ends soon.*
And then, a dead fish.
Sometimes, we fight our way out
and sometimes, we fold in.

In fake Montreal, because I talked
you out of real Montreal, there was a girl
on a dance floor and you fell

in love right in front of me.
And this was the end— not
what you said on the bed.

And most Decembers, you'll say
you love me. And most Decembers,
I won't believe you.

CAN I MAKE YOU MY COLOSSUS?

This is the accident I never see:
maybe it is my fault— but I think,
just because I do this all the time,
it doesn't mean anything to me—

I'll craft the song and drink
the wine, create the scene
like I care, and I will believe it.
It'll feel fucked up and real.

You'll tell me the story about a woman
who thought you'd leave your fiancé—
who snapped one day and stayed up
all night, broke up with her live-in
boyfriend. She dragged you
into a conference room.

Even though you'd told her,
*one day, I'll just disengage
and that'll be it— it'll be over.*

And you will use that—
it will become mantra.

And this is the place for you
and me. We're tough.

The front seat of a borrowed car—
The Psychedelic Furs:

There's a song on the air
with a love-you line

You regret telling me
about the conference room.

This is the scene: you are screaming
on a beach, narrowly avoiding fist fights
that you incited in the first place,
while assuring me that I am not
in the wrong in my own conference
room moment, that I'm not *at all like her*.
That this other guy is a pussy
because he could not act.
But it's just a collection of small
moments: a hand on the small
of the back, legs interlocked
on a hammock. My knees between
yours, a bar stool, yelling out a hotel
window at teenagers in a parking lot.

I'm just mining for heartbreak.
Chipping away, looking for cheap metal—
anything that won't hold up,
anything to displace blame.

A sliver of neck tattoo, someone
who places the wrong emphasis
on the *S* syllable of a word.

IF THERE IS SOMETHING THAT ILLUSTRATES THE DIFFERENCE BETWEEN YOU AND ME, IT'S THIS

At the wine bar—
the man with the size thirty-four
sticker still on the leg of his pants—
I want to tell him and you won't let me;
instead, we take a picture.

You insist that everything
is going to be okay as the lines
on my chest x-ray draw themselves
deeper, showing up now
where they were not before.

I insist that everything
will be okay if your definition
of okay includes a choice between
puffy-faced or exhaustion,
coughing up blood or missing a night out

where I could be sixteen again
for a minute, lost in the music,
dancing and talking shit, smoking
cloves and staying late
after the show to buy records.

But if this is okay, or at least what's
between me and not okay—
then let it be punctuated with rosé

and oysters served with a trio of sauces:
cocktail, horseradish, and minuet.

Let there be a comfortable chair
in a hotel lobby that offers
Snack Pack pudding—
the kind that doesn't need
refrigeration and never goes bad.

BESIDES THE ONES WHERE WE'VE BEEN

If there were new places for us,
I would think they'd have hammocks,
putting our faces inches apart,
smooshing us closer together.

There would be streetlights and we'd dance,
even if we'd have to stop for cars,
even if neither of us liked the song.

Grooves worn and set— the places
we've been rubbed raw,
turning slow, grating circles.

The unintelligible point we never get to
(the middle of the night text)

We always send, but promptly forget
the cryptic message.

In backyards, we regret losing—
the letters we burned on a gas grill.

Like the perfect black ink on your bare back,
I'd want the new places to stand out.

I'd want to them to shimmer, like washing
the words off and forgetting they were there.

No matter how hard we tried, I'd want
them to be places we could never get back to.
I'd want them to be unfathomable.

FIRE ANTS

"In a room, all I feel is the cold that you left."
                                                                —*The Red House Painters*

Every one of your stories starts with—
I spent four nights in jail in that city.
And it's never your fault, really.

In Ohio, you spent three nights locked up
with a fractured skull.

Your eyesight was gone for six months,
you still don't have a strong sense of smell.
Now, ice cream tastes like freezer burn.

You told me sometimes you smell
something you recognize as me,
even when I'm not around.

Perhaps it's scent spirits I've left
to haunt you— a mixture
of hair products and wine.

You're on your way to New Mexico
and I've discovered fire ants,
while walking the dog in a Texas field.

Each one I squish on my skin leaves
a small, burning speck—
a red, stinging afterthought.

BATHTUBS AND BACKYARDS

You came here for simple things
you thought would make everything better—
bathtubs and driveways and backyards.

But you never use these things.
Never soak in the bath
or swing in the hammock or rock
in the chair you coveted
for years and finally bought.

No, you reminisce over mix CDs stacked
on a spindle, flip through until you find
the ones with the handwriting
that isn't yours, the ones men gave you.

Some handwriting you remember,
even after decades. You only identify more
recent ones by a process of elimination.

If the muscles ached when you were younger,
if it became hard to breathe, it wasn't
because it was actually harder.
It was something in your head.

Or it just was. The way the bathwater rises
too high when forgotten.

IN THE WAITING ROOM OF THE DELL CHILDREN'S HOSPITAL CF CLINIC AT AGE FORTY

The Disney princess pictures and *Finding Nemo* posters
                haphazardly   tacked up
         at registration cubicles   where
               nurses   wearing cartoon scrubs
       remind you   of the fact that
    you are supposed to be dead by now.

Even your medicine   reeks of   childhood:

           Asian hamsters.

Imagine.   A tiny syringe   extracting
secretions   from their genetically   engineered ovaries.

              Remember that fragile hamster
              you owned for three days?
                        It caught
                        cold and died.

So many dead hamsters.
             Their tiny bodies
             cooling off

water removed
from flame.

But that one death?

You cried. More than
all the others.

Not because you
knew it best.

You loved it best

because
it was the most

beautiful.

Is there some kind of strange beauty   in slowly   dying
of a child's disease,
but not knowing until decades later?

You never got out
of gym class or to Make-A-Wish to meet Damien Rice
or topped the other girls'
sob stories at Whitney Shumate's
sleepover when they kept playing
Richard Marx's *Hold on to the Nights* and crying.

How do we explain something that took us by surprise?

Now, you can't remember if you had nothing
to share   because
you're not   really
a joiner   or because you walked in
late   and they were already
crying.

THIS IS HOW IT IS

*for Matthew who was kind enough to share his "nerd journal" with
me*

In the young adult book-turned-movie
about my disease, they keep
describing the tubing, how the main
character still looks *cute*
even with cannula up her nose.

The author labors over vials of hypertonic saline
and strategically organized med carts
with cupfuls of Creon, pages
of Flovents and Afflovests
to ensure authenticity.

When they kill the unnecessary
character to prove that the disease
is terminal, he is just a slight blue on the floor,
unmoving while the nurse weeps over his body.

But there are only two mentions of phlegm,
and even those are treated like delicate
renderings— nothing deep green
or thick or bloody or draining
down someone's face. Or coughed
up so hard the patient vomits
all over themselves while sitting in traffic.

I wonder why there is no scene where the main
character shits herself while using her shaky
vest and has to shower and clean her sheets
before rushing to work where her student
shows her his "nerd journal" where he catalogues
the daily care and lives of his tropical fish.

And I think, yes, this is how it is,
as I read his description of a molting
porcelain crab who is swarmed
by Nassarius snails because they smell
death and so they rip both claws
from his soft-shelled body.

THE EVER-PRESENT PINK SKY

In a coffee shop,
a man says
the girls
at his daughter's
kindergarten are

slicing each other up.

One minute, Suzie
is her best friend
and the next,

she's over it.

The boys,
they start then—
one day, she's all
about Liam and Solomon.
And the next,

they're over
Liam and Solomon.

In poems,
God's hand reaches
into your puppet body
before you die.
You have no control.

Somewhere on a balcony
of a once-glorious hotel,
now with toilets
that run too long,

you're trying to find where
a relationship ends.

At your feet, neon pink
Mardi Gras beads,
a discarded plastic tiara.

Crickets,
dead in corners—
beautiful
crystalized shells.

You try to relish
cracked paint on doors.

And shouldn't cracked paint
be enough?

Something splintered
from its intention
to stunning pattern.

Having children
makes you think
of your own mortality.

And I think, dying
makes you think
of your own mortality.

DESERT TAROT

and this is where
people come
to forget
their mothers

we envy darkness
noble, devilish
in its necessity

leaves like tap
dancers, skittered
across stone slabs
landed at the feet
of strange cacti

we are blind
powerless
in this blaze

your grace failed
when you needed
to bury a memory
in a shallow
grave in West Texas

we are burnt
limitless
in our catharsis

you delved too far
reoriented yourself
beneath too much sky
saw everything
it contained

a cup held
by a hand
that reached
from heavens
and stretched
warnings
in the offing

we are not
the salamander
who can pass through
fire unscathed

but each cloud
contained wings
and you intend
to wear a crown
of your haunted
thoughts

WITH GRATITUDE

There is no way I can properly express my gratitude to the following people who helped make this collection possible. First and foremost, thank you to Judy Jensen and Tina Posner, whose suggestions and edits made this something worth publishing and to the rest of the Brass Tacks critique group for their guidance and support over the past decade. There would be no poems without you. To Wendy Duren, Tod Goldberg, and Jill Alexander Essbaum whose friendship, faith, and support I may not be worthy of, but I will always treasure. All of my gratitude to my teachers over the years who really saw me and whose care allowed me to think I had something inside worth saying: Mary MacNeil, Wendy Matheson, Cameron L. Marzelli, Aron Keesbury, Joe Osterhaus, Jason Shinder, Timothy Liu, Ed Ochester, and most of all Bonnie Staiger. Thank you to Sandra Matson, Whitney Shumate, Jessica Piazza and Al Haney, who listened to my concerns and offered support along the way. To my dear former students Alysia Thomas and Matthew Musat who sparked poems and Ceschi Ramos whose music not only worked its way into some lines but also inspired me along the way. So many thanks to my dear and benevolent friend, Johnny Northrup, who sat at my kitchen table and workshopped poems with me when we were just teenagers. You were my first critique partner and my chosen family. Love you Big Shoots. Thank you to my family and friends who have encouraged me over the years, especially Chelsea McCaffrey who got Tyler B. Johnston to congratulate me on this acceptance. Thank you to the Writing Room of Boston who gave me space to complete an earlier draft of this chapbook and to all the journals that first published these poems. And most especially thank you to my editor and the rest of the team at Unsolicited

Press for making this happen for me. And finally, thank you to Dr. Sean Gilbey who diagnosed me with Cystic Fibrosis after decades of unanswered questions, the team at the Dell Children's CF clinic in Austin, and Vertex, the makers of the drug Trikafta, all of whom made it so I might no longer be the dying girl.

ACKNOWLEDGEMENTS

"Fire Ants" originally appeared in *La Fovea*

The poem "Looking at a friend's photographs of the Salton Sea the morning after he killed himself" originally appeared in the journal *Blood and Bourbon Spring 2017*

The poems "In the Waiting Room of the Dell Children's Hospital CF Clinic at Age Forty" and "A few seconds to answer" originally appeared in *The Coachella Review Summer 2017*

The poems "The Lobster" and "Providence" originally appeared in *Two Hawks Quarterly Spring 2017*

The poems "If there is something that illustrates the difference between me and you, it's this" and "Bathtubs and backyards" originally appeared in *The Windward Review Vol. 16*

The poems "Besides the ones we've been," "The ever-living ghost of what once was," and "Maine/ Montreal" originally appeared in *Shelia-Na-Gig Volume 3.3 Spring 2019*

The poem "Agapitós" originally appeared in *The Ear May 2019*

The poem "A litany of bad decisions" originally appeared in *2River May 2019*

The poems "This is How it Is" and "The ever-present pink sky" originally appeared in *The Lake February 2020*

The poem "The split second where it begins and splinters outward" originally appeared in *The Phoenix* Spring 2020.

ABOUT THE AUTHOR

Bree Rolfe lives in Austin, TX where she teaches writing and literature to the mostly reluctant, but always loveable, teenagers at James Bowie High School. Her work has appeared in Saul Williams' poetry anthology *Chorus: A Literary Mixtape*, the Barefoot Muse Anthology *Forgetting Home: Poems About Alzheimer's*, the Redpaint Hill Anthology *Mother is a Verb*, and 5AM Magazine. She holds an MFA from the Writing Seminars at Bennington College.